**DO NOT REMOVE
CARDS FROM POCKET**

Racing Yesterday's Cars

Racing Yesterday's Cars

RICHARD L. KNUDSON

 Lerner Publications Company • Minneapolis, Minnesota

ACKNOWLEDGMENTS: All of the photographs in this book have been provided by the author with the exception of the following: pp. 32, 33, Phil Prowse.

LIBRARY OF CONGRESS CATALOGING-IN-PUBLICATION DATA

Knudson, Richard L.
 Racing yesterday's cars.

 (Superwheels & thrill sports)
 Summary: Discusses the sport of vintage car racing describing its history, the cars used, the different types of races, safety, and rules. Also gives information on how to find and restore a vintage car and the names of vintage racing clubs.
  1. Automobile racing—United States—History—Juvenile literature. 2. Automobiles, Racing—History—Juvenile literature. [1. Automobile racing. 2. Automobiles, Racing] I. Title. II. Series.
 GV1033.K68 1986   796.7'2'0973   85-24006
 ISBN 0-8225-0512-6 (lib. bdg.)

Manufactured in the United States of America

International Standard Book Number: 0-8225-0512-6
Library of Congress Catalog Card Number: 85-24006

1 2 3 4 5 6 7 8 9 10 94 93 92 91 90 89 88 87 86

Drivers of three blue Bugattis, a red M.G., and several other restored classics await the start of a hillclimb event (see page 22).

CONTENTS

Bugattis may have won more sports car races than any other model.

THE THRILL OF RACING

Whether on foot, on horseback, or in some sort of vehicle, the sport of racing has challenged and excited people for centuries. In the late 1800s, the invention of the automobile brought much faster speeds, which made racing even more thrilling.

Unfortunately for most would-be racers, today's sleek racing cars are very expensive and often require further streamlining at huge added costs. Luckily, however, there is still a way for people with limited budgets to participate in automobile racing, and that is by racing a *vintage* car. (When speaking of cars, the word "vintage" refers to an older car that has not been modernized but is in, or has been, restored to its original state.)

Unlike the more popular kinds of automobile racing that offer prize money or trophies, vintage racing is organized purely for fun. To participate, one needs only to have an old car and plenty of enthusiasm.

A Bugatti touring car rounds a hairpin turn.

This homemade midget racer *(front)* has a Ford Model-A engine. The car behind it is a Willys championship ("Indy") car.

HOW VINTAGE CAR RACING BEGAN

The sport of racing vintage cars began in England in 1934 when a group of Englishmen organized the Vintage Sports Car Club (VSCC). The club's first race was held at Donington Park on July 10, 1937, and the competition included several Bugattis, an Aston Martin, and a Mercedes-Benz. Today, the English VSCC has more than 6,000 members and sponsors many races each year.

After World War II, vintage car racing gradually spread to the United States. U.S. servicemen who were stationed in Great Britain during the 1940s had discovered the English sports car. They were especially attracted to the jaunty M.G., a small two-seater with long, graceful fenders and wire-spoked wheels. Because of its excellent suspension system, the M.G. had unusually good cornering ability and could be driven quickly, yet safely — even over narrow, winding roads.

After the war, many M.G.s were imported to the United States. Sports car fever soared, and before long car clubs were formed and the first vintage sports car races were held. Today, both British and North American racers are enthusiastic about attending vintage racing events.

Although vintage racing is a popular sport in both Great Britain and in North America, at first glance, it may seem that the British are more serious about the sport. Races are held more frequently in England and, because the country is small, distances between race courses are not great. In the United States, however, race courses are hundreds of miles apart, which makes it more difficult and expensive for participants to attend racing events.

A 1935 M.G. racer. The M.G. sparked interest in sport cars in the United States and led to the development of the Chevrolet Corvette and the Ford Thunderbird in the early 1950s.

In a race, the British often drive their cars harder and faster than North Americans do. One reason may be that it is easier for British drivers to find spare parts for their cars because so many of them were manufactured in England. In contrast, drivers who race old English sports cars in the United States have to be more cautious. They are probably every bit as serious about the sport, but they also want to race again—and soon. Therefore, they don't want to risk losing or damaging a part that might take six months or more to replace.

With its front headlights taped for safety, a restored 1931 M.G. M Type Midget is closely followed by another M.G. that is almost as old. The two-seater M Type was the first M.G. to be mass-produced; 3,200 were built between 1928 and 1932.

This fenderless 1931 Model-A Ford jalopy (*right*) and 1957 Ford V-8 (*left*) are both popular vintage race cars.

VINTAGE RACE CARS

Although a large number of vintage cars still exist, not every old car is best suited for racing. For instance, some restored *antique* (any car that is older than 25 years) and *classic* (a high-quality car produced between 1925 and 1948) cars are better suited for collections, for limited personal driving on special occasions, and for exhibition at car shows. Vintage cars that are used for racing usually fall into one of the following four categories: *jalopies and stock cars, sprint and midget cars, sports cars,* and *championship ("Indy") cars.*

JALOPIES AND STOCK CARS

In the 1930s, at countless county fairgrounds across the United States, *jalopies* provided entertainment for millions of racing fans. A jalopy racer usually started as a dilapidated Ford or Chevrolet coupe from the early or mid-1930s. Its fenders were cut down and extra weight removed, braces were welded in around the radiator and the doors, and the engine was rebuilt and "souped up" for extra performance. Today, many of these old jalopies—the forerunner of today's power-packed stock cars—are now being found and restored for racing.

Stock cars are ordinary-looking production cars with powerful engines that were built especially for racing. Sometimes they were rebuilt from old engines, often from 1933 Ford V-8s. In the United States, stock car racing is especially popular in the South.

Even though stock car bodies are strengthened with steel pipes, breakdowns often happen during a race because the super-tuned engine puts a great strain on the car's gears, suspension system, and wheels.

These restored 1930s dirt track sprinters, modeled after ''Indy'' racers, raise plenty of dust.

SPRINT AND MIDGET CARS

Sprint racing on dirt tracks provides breathtaking, top-speed action from start to finish. Before certain safety precautions were required, *sprint car* racing was the most dangerous of all automotive sports.

While designed to race on shorter tracks of 50 laps or less, sprint cars are similar to the "Indy" race cars of the 1930s and 1940s. Their *chassis* (frame) was built by cutting down the frame of a passenger car, usually a 1930s Ford. The car had an open cockpit, fenderless wheels, and a slender front hood that tapered almost to a point. It was most often powered by a Ford engine, and extra equipment was added to the engine to boost the car's performance. Since the late 1960s, a bulky *roll cage* (a safety device to protect the driver during rolls) has been required equipment on all sprint cars.

Because sprint cars perform better at peak RPM (run at top speed) throughout a race, they often go into turns in a right-angle maneuver known as *broadsliding*. Bumping, sudden *spinouts* (loss of control and turning end for end), chain-reaction pile-ups, and spectacular flips are common occurrances in sprint racing.

A smaller version of the sprint car is the *midget*. Like sprint cars, midgets were built from existing car parts that had been cut down. The *track* (width) of a midget was 41 inches, and the *wheelbase* (distance from the center of the front wheel to the center of the rear wheel) measured 74 inches.

15

A highly prized Kurtis-Kraft midget racer. Frank Kurtis built more than 2,000 of these popular little racing machines.

Midget racing began in the 1930s. At first, most midget racers were homemade. But after World War II, Frank Kurtis, a car builder living in California, began to produce midget racers on an assembly line. The sport became so popular that Kurtis quickly sold 1,000 cars. Although Kurtis may be better known for designing the low roadster that set the styling trend for Indianapolis 500 racers, his midget racer established him as the best race car builder in the United States.

Because they were so common in their day, midgets are easier to find than many other types of vintage cars, and they make up the majority of entrants at most old car races.

A group of midget racers. These scaled-down "Indy" cars were designed for racing on short tracks.

Led by a blue Bugatti, a green Lester M.G. *(left)* **and a red Aston Martin** *(right)* **line up for a left-hand turn.**

SPORTS CARS

Since the early 1930s, automakers in Europe and in the United States have produced many different kinds of *sports cars*. Most of them are low and rather small, usually two-seaters, and are designed for quick response, easy maneuverability, and high-speed driving. Today, older sports cars such as the M.G., Austin-Healey, Frazer Nash, Corvette, Bugatti, Morgan, Bently, Vauxhall, and Amilcar are raced. Some of these cars are quite rare, however, and are not often seen at U.S. races. Although owners of vintage sports cars like to "open them up" in a race to demonstrate how fast they can go, they are always careful not to take any foolish chances with their valuable automobiles.

CHAMPIONSHIP ("INDY") CARS

Championship cars (also called "Indy cars") are race cars that were built especially for the Indianapolis 500 and other races for the American Automobile Association (AAA) championship. Many of them are well known because of their drivers or the races they won. Although Indy cars look very much like the smaller sprint and midget cars, their inner workings are more complex.

Indy cars are the most expensive of all vintage cars, and the few that have been restored are usually brought out only for shows or for demonstration runs. As more and more of these cars are made "track-ready," however, no doubt they will once again be seen in competition with each other.

A driver begins the winding and challenging Vintage Prescott hillclimb course.

KINDS OF VINTAGE CAR RACING

The two main kinds of vintage car racing—*road racing* and *oval-track racing*—are different in several ways.

ROAD RACING

The first major sports car race in the United States was held on a marked-off route along the city streets and rural roads of Watkins Glen, New York, in October 1948. Organized by a sports car enthusiast named Cameron Artginsinger, the Watkins Glen Grand Prix brought dozens of sports cars to the starting line as thousands watched and cheered. The race was a great success, and other races soon followed.

In Europe, it was common to stage car races on country roads between two towns. These popular city-to-city road races included hills as well as both right and left turns. Sports cars and European *formula cars* (single seaters without fenders and built to conform to an international set of rules) were best suited to this form of racing.

Even when the road was closed to regular traffic, racing cars on the open road was risky. Because of the danger, racing on public highways was outlawed in most of the United States in the mid-1950s. Instead, sports car racing continued on artificial road courses that were constructed throughout the country. Today, several major U.S. cities—Los Angeles, Las Vegas, Cleveland, and Detroit—again allow Grand Prix races to be held on their closed-off city streets, and other cities may follow.

Sports cars also compete in another kind of road racing called *"hillclimbing."* Following a preset route, cars race up a hill, one at a time, and the driver who reaches the top in the shortest time wins the event. Depending on the course, hillclimbing can be safer than racing with a group of cars because there is no danger of colliding with another car. Drivers, however, do have to be alert for trees and rocks near the edge of the road.

Pike's Peak, a mountain in Colorado, is the site of one famous annual hillclimbing event in the United States. Another well-known course, the Vintage Prescott, is located in England. The short Prescott climb challenges cars and drivers with a tough test and provides lots of excitement for spectators.

Two Bugattis—a fenderless Grand Prix two-seater racer (*left*) and a touring car (*right*)—compete on an oval track.

OVAL-TRACK RACING

While many countries continued to enjoy set-route racing on open roads, the United States soon turned to oval-track racing. Oval tracks, flat and with left turns only, are perhaps less dangerous than open-road racing. One of the earliest U.S. oval tracks was built in Indianapolis, Indiana. A famous 500-mile race—the Indianapolis (Indy) 500— has been held there every Memorial Day since 1911. Although not as well known as the Indy course, other oval tracks have been built across the country.

At a typical oval track, the area located just off the track near the starting line is called the *"pits."* There is one pit area for each race car, and it is where the mechanics and crew members refuel and repair cars during a race.

The *paddock* is an infield parking area near the pits and the starting line. Here owners give their cars a final check before the starting flag. The paddock area is sometimes open to the public, and it is a fascinating place to be before the competition begins. At some of the larger races, the many vintage cars gathered in the paddock offer spectators a rare closeup look at automotive history.

While most oval-track racing is done on a smooth, paved surface, sprint cars are usually raced on dirt tracks. Appropriately named "dusty heroes," sprint car drivers often have to pilot their cars through flying dust and dirt, and spectators, too, usually go home

A "dusty hero" rounds the track.

covered with dust. The sight of four or five sprint cars coming around a corner at full speed and kicking up a dense cloud of dust behind them is difficult to describe but impressive to see. Add to the dust and the dirt the ear-splitting roar of unmuffled engines, and one begins to catch the flavor of the event!

Rather than everyone starting at once—called a *"massed start"*—some vintage races are staged as *"handicap"* events. In such competitions, some cars start ahead of the others, with the slowest car starting first. The actual spacing between cars—calculated in seconds—is based on the performance of each car and driver in earlier races.

Sometimes, the fastest car in a handicap race does not start until the first, or slowest, cars have already finished two or three laps. Handicap races are exciting to watch because the last cars to start are usually passing other cars throughout the race. If the people who assigned the handicaps have done their job well, all of the cars should cross the finish line at almost the same time. This possibility adds a thrilling climax to an already fast-moving race.

Sometimes a sprint driver encounters more mud than dust!

This Model-A Ford coupe may have been found behind someone's barn.

FINDING A VINTAGE CAR

Believe it or not, old racing cars *do* hide behind country barns. Although a valuable car like a Bugatti probably won't be found hiding in the weeds, an old Ford stock car from the 1950s or 1960s just might be there. And such a car is a true vintage racing car.

The United States is dotted with race tracks, and the small towns near these tracks can be great places to look for old cars. Asking about vintage cars at garages and gas stations that have been in business for a long time can also provide some useful leads. Also check old newspapers at the local public library for names of drivers who raced in years past. Then, with the help of a telephone book, try to locate and meet some of the people mentioned in the newspaper, as they might still have a car or some early racing equipment or know of some other old-timers who do.

Joining a vintage car club is another excellent way to gain help in finding a car. Most clubs publish a magazine or newsletter that advertises cars for sale as well as cars that people want to buy. People at club meetings and at races and shows will also often be able to produce leads to finding just the right vintage car.

In addition, there are also several auto magazines that regularly feature advertisements for antique race cars that are for sale. They include the following publications:

Joining a vintage car club provides opportunities to search for old cars or needed parts, as the man wearing a sign listing the parts he is looking for is doing.

Antique Motor News
919 South Street
Long Beach, CA 90805

Car Classics & Car Collector
P.O. Box 28571
Atlanta, GA 30228

Cars & Parts
Box 150
Sidney, OH 45365

Hemmings Motor News
Box 100
Bennington, VT 05201

Old Cars Weekly Newspaper
700 East State Street
Iola, IA 54945

Success in locating a vintage car depends on making as many contacts as possible. Never stop searching. Finding a car and authentic spare parts and discovering its history can be both intriguing and a lot of fun.

Some cars are not restored but are raced in the condition in which they were found.

Two early M.G.s await restoration. M.G.s have separate bodies and chassis and are easier to restore than unibody models, which are built with the body and the chassis as one unit.

RESTORING A VINTAGE CAR

Once a vintage car has been found, it must be *restored* (brought back) to racing condition. Safety is of greatest importance, so both the car's steering and suspension systems must be almost entirely dismantled. Then each dismantled part must be carefully examined and cleaned and rebuilt.

Before taking anything apart, take photographs of the car from every angle. Also make some rough sketches to show the location of each part that is removed, how the parts are connected to each other, and in what order they should be reassembled. The photos and sketches will prove to be invaluable when the car is ready to be put back together again.

After a thorough cleaning, each part should be painted, and some major parts, such as the steering arms and spindles, must be *magnafluxed* (a process used to detect cracks and weak points in steel). All worn bushings and bearings, brake linings, cylinders, and hoses should be replaced, and the chassis, axles, and various parts of the running gear should be cleaned, inspected, and painted.

Even if the car is not scheduled for completion right away, any parts that need to be chrome plated should be sent out immediately. Rechroming can take a long time, and prices for the work have been steadily increasing.

The engine, of course, must be inspected very closely. Replace all worn parts, and then clean and paint it. It is necessary to have a dependable engine that performs well, but avoid overdoing work on the engine. Many "souped-up" items that increase the engine's power and efficiency will also make it difficult to tune and will create too much trouble for pleasurable vintage racing.

This man is making a pattern for a Mercedes SSK trunk lid from wood. He will form the metal for the lid around the wood for a perfect fit and will then attach the metal lid to the car.

To restore the car's body, remove all of the old paint, weld the cracks, and smooth out any dents. Do the final painting and any numbering or lettering only after learning about the car's original color and markings. Restoring the car to duplicate the way it looked when it was new—what color it was painted, what number appeared on its tail, and what *accessories* (extra equipment) it had—greatly increases its uniqueness and value. Also try to track down as much of the car's history as possible— its past owners and drivers, when and where the car was raced, and the racing results— because a vintage car with a known history is more valuable than one about which nothing is known.

Everyone, of course, wants a nice looking car, and the process of restoration will lead to dramatic improvements in a car's appearance. The goal of a successful restoration, however, should be to match the car's original appearance as closely as possible without going beyond

In this busy warehouse, handsome vintage cars such as this row of Bugattis are slowly being rebuilt, piece by piece. While some of these valuable classics will be raced, others will only be displayed and used for private driving.

A nicely restored Kurtis-Kraft midget racer

what is practical or appropriate. Over-restoration can be a problem for many first-time restorers, and mastering the art of true restoration comes with experience and knowing that the time to stop is the first-time that everything looks "just right."

Over-restoration also costs a great deal of extra money and can make an owner reluctant to race the restored car for fear of damaging it. While exhibiting a restored car at antique car shows can be enjoyable, the real fun in owning a vintage race car is entering it in various racing events. Museum pieces belong in museums, but race cars belong on the track!

SAFETY

In keeping with the spirit of vintage racing and to avoid unnecessary accidents, owners of vintage race cars do not add modern equipment when restoring, modifying, or repairing their cars. For example, rather than making adjustments so today's wider tires can be used, a restorer will instead use narrow tires exactly like those that were originally on the car. Although wider tires would improve the car's cornering ability, it would also cause stress to and would eventually damage the car's suspension and steering systems. The narrow tires are, therefore, both more authentic and also safer.

Sometimes, a compromise can be made between the old and the new to allow for both safety and the desire to preserve the old-time character of vintage car racing. For example, although drivers must now wear fireproof driving suits and leather shoes when on the track, they will often arrive wearing colorful shirts, jackets, and hats dating from the time when their cars were manufactured. Drivers of English cars often wear tweed coats and Deerstalker ("Sherlock Holmes") hats. Leather flying helmets from World War I are also popular.

Vintage car clubs stress safety for all of their members. When racing, drivers are required to wear helmets of top-quality material. Every helmet must display the "Snell 80" sticker of approval, which means it has passed a rigid safety test. Drivers must use both a safety harness and a securely mounted seatbelt. Although most clubs do not enforce their use, roll bars and *safety cages* (a tubular steel structure surrounding the driver's seat) are also recommended to protect the driver in case of an accident or rollover. Many racing clubs now require the magnafluxing of critical car parts, such as front spindles, axles, and steering parts.

Roll bars were first added to sprint cars for safety in the late 1960s.

Perhaps the greatest safety factor in racing, however, is the race car driver's mental attitude The majority of the drivers are racing for fun and not for cutthroat competitiveness. They respect each other and the power of their machines. And because of the difficulty and the cost of finding replacement parts, the last thing they want to do is to damage or destroy their cars.

At all vintage racing events, every car must undergo a complete inspection before the race. Qualified inspectors check each car to be sure it meets the rules and specifications for the upcoming race, and they also look for anything that could cause a hazard on the track and endanger other cars and drivers. This inspection is called *"scrutineering,"* and the inspectors are *"scrutineers."*

Drivers are required to wear an approved helmet and fireproofed clothing.

Most clubs require that beginning drivers complete some degree of training before they are allowed to race. Sometimes, this training is as simple as being observed while completing several laps around the track. At other times, the training may involve attending a weekend driver's school. Often a beginning racer's car is identified by a brightly colored "X" next to the race number. When more experienced and faster drivers see the "X," they try to give the novice plenty of room on the track.

The "Midnight Riley Special," a modified "Indy" racer, is a consistent winner at antique automobile shows.

VINTAGE RACING CLUBS

There are many clubs that promote and sponsor vintage racing, and all of them operate in a way that encourages good sportsmanship among racing enthusiasts. To be eligible to race in most clubs, a car must be at least 15 or 20 years old and be "unmodernized," or restored to the way it was when it was raced as a new car. Other eligibility rules vary, so interested drivers must check the rules of each individual club.

The oldest vintage racing club in the United States, the Vintage Sports Car Club of America (VSCCA), was organized in 1959. Similar to the VSCC in England, the U.S. club sponsors vintage races at Lime Rock, Connecticut; Bryar, New Hampshire; and Watkins Glen, New York. These sites have artificial road courses—closed circuits that include hills and all sorts of right and left turns. Most vintage sports cars, formula cars, and *special cars* (modified production sports cars) that were built or raced before 1959 are eligible for competition at VSCCA events, and they are usually raced in classes according to their engine size. All pre-World War II cars usually race against each other, however, because they are fewer in number. The VSCCA also sponsors hillclimbing events.

Another U.S. club organized for vintage racing cars is the Antique Automobile Racing Association (AARA). Founded in 1973, the AARA has two primary goals: to promote the use and enjoyment of its members' cars and to preserve the history of dirt track racing in the United States. AARA races are almost always held on dirt tracks and often seem more like shows than races. The cars circle in fast laps in close groups with the lead changing frequently, but this changing of positions is not really a clue as to who is "winning." Instead, the shifts are usually made only for the benefit of the crowd.

"The Masked Marvel" has appeared at dirt track races since the 1930s. Here a modern-day "Marvel" speeds around the track wearing a blackened-out face shield.

Just as in the earlier days of racing, clowns and other entertainment are often featured at AARA meets. One popular event is the appearance of "The Masked Marvel." Alone on the track, a driver attempts to complete several high-speed laps while blindfolded. It's a breathtaking show that thrills the spectators.

The Atlantic Coast Old Timers' Auto Racing Club (ACOTARC) is yet another vintage racing club. A large club with enthusiastic members, the ACOTARC holds races on various tracks in the eastern United States and sponsors events similar to those of the AARA. And like the AARA, it often provides entertainment between races.

Most tracks with a fairly long history will have some kind of local old-timers club that sponsors events for cars that raced at the track in past years. The club also helps to research and preserve the history of their particular track.

Throughout the United States, there are also many local and regional vintage racing clubs. Joining such clubs will provide opportunities for meeting others who are interested in vintage racing and to keep up on new developments in this colorful and exciting hobby.

Antique Automobile Racing
     Association (AARA)
Box 116
Ixonia, WI 53036

Atlantic Coast Old Timers'
     Auto Racing Club (ACOTARC)
Box 3067
Alexandria, VA 22302

Vintage Sports Car Club
     of America, Inc. (VSCCA)
170 Wetherhill Road
Garden City, NY 11530

A line-up of midget race cars ready to perform

After this midget racer has been inspected and declared to be "race ready," it will be driven back to the paddock.

LET'S GO RACING!

Now that your car has been restored, you probably want to race it. So let's go to a VSCCA event at Lime Rock, Connecticut. Since you're new on the vintage racing scene, we'll take in the season opener in April. That first race of the year also includes a drivers' school, which is required of all new drivers.

A four-wheeled trailer is the best means of transporting a car to the track. Once the car is squarely on the trailer, it must be securely tied down. During travel, the car's transmission should be put in neutral so that the motion of the car will not cause wear on the gears.

Traveling to the track with a gleaming restored car will often bring inquiring looks from people who are passed on the way. Sometimes you'll even get a big smile and a cheerful "thumbs up" from people who admire old cars.

At the gate, all drivers and crewpeople must register for the event and sign release forms. The release form protects the organizing club and the track owners from possible law suits if an accident occurs.

After signing in, we go to the paddock where we unload the car and set up a work space. Since the car is ready to race, there should not be much work to do on it at the beginning of the day. However, some mechanical problems might pop up later. After the car has been unloaded, it is taken through *tech* (technical inspection, or scrutinering). The inspectors will want to see the driver's suit, gloves, and helmet and will also inspect the car for any mechanical defects.

We put the driver's equipment in the car and push it over to the tech inspection garage.

The paddock area is a fascinating place to be before the race. Some of the racers have already been parked at track side and others are still being brought in.

After all of the safety equipment has been checked, the inspectors look for leaks in the lubrication, fuel, and cooling systems. The level of brake fluid is verified, and the car's front is jacked up to check its suspension and steering systems.

When the inspectors are satisfied, they put a special sticker on the car's roll bar to certify that it is race worthy. Next, it's over to the pumps to take on a few gallons of racing gasoline. At about $3.50 a gallon, there's no need to fill up! Besides, the extra weight might slow you down.

Back in your paddock space and ready to go, you now have some time to walk around and see the other beautiful cars that will be raced. There are gorgeous blue Bugattis, green Jaguars and Bentleys, red Ferraris, and other examples of almost every kind of sports car ever built. Everyone is friendly and has a kind word. Cameras click from every direction as this gathering of newly rebuilt and polished cars brings delight to the many enthusiastic viewers.

An announcer's voice soon booms over the public address system: "All student drivers are now to report to the timing tower for instructions." Some of the seasoned drivers hold a blackboard session to show you and other new racers the best way around the track. They explain that every turn has an *apex* (outermost point), and that the quickest and safest way through a turn is to come as close to that point as possible while using as much of the track as necessary before and after reaching the apex.

A variety of vintage sports cars, including a white Jaguar *(left)*, a red Italian-made Siata *(center)*, and a trailing red Formula Junior, leave the pit area for a practice run. Behind the Siata is an unpainted Porsche.

Now you and the other student drivers are allowed to walk the track in order to study the correct lines through a turn and to examine the road surface. Once that lap on foot has been completed, the track is opened to experienced drivers. You and the other student drivers are grouped on various corners, each with an instructor, to watch the way the drivers maneuver through the turns. After observing on every corner, you and the other students are ready to try it yourselves. The announcement, "The track is now open for student practice," comes none too soon for the anxious new drivers.

After all of your safety gear is on and your seat belt is securely fastened, the marshall at the end of pit row waves you out on to the track. The first laps are thrilling, but a bit frightening, too. Since this road course is almost two miles long, it's easy to forget what comes next. In fact, near the top of a few of the hills, the next turns are not yet visible, so it takes a good deal of concentration to decide in which direction to begin turning. You also have the problem of selecting the proper moment for downshifting and choosing the correct gear to keep your engine racing.

Before long, you realize that the combination of blackboard instruction and walking the track has really helped you to find the right line through the turns, and you hit the apex almost every time. Then, after what seems like a very short time, you spot the checkered flag being waved, which signals the end of practice. At the end of the next lap, you raise your hand, turn into the pit lane, and return to your paddock spot.

It's lunchtime. You mingle with the others, and you enjoy hearing encouraging words from the experienced drivers about your driving. The race went well, and all of those months of hard work restoring and preparing your car have paid off. Now you're a vintage racer!

Superwheels & Thrill Sports

Airplanes
AEROBATICS
AIRPLANE RACING
FLYING-MODEL AIRPLANES
HELICOPTERS
HOME-BUILT AIRPLANES
PERSONAL AIRPLANES
RECORD-BREAKING AIRPLANES
SCALE-MODEL AIRPLANES
YESTERDAY'S AIRPLANES
UNUSUAL AIRPLANES

Automobiles & Auto Racing
AMERICAN RACE CAR DRIVERS
THE DAYTONA 500
DRAG RACING
ICE RACING
THE INDIANAPOLIS 500
INTERNATIONAL RACE CAR DRIVERS
LAND SPEED RECORD BREAKERS
RACING YESTERDAY'S CARS
RALLYING
ROAD RACING
TRACK RACING

CLASSIC SPORTS CARS
CUSTOM CARS
DINOSAUR CARS: LATE GREAT CARS
   FROM 1945 TO 1966

FABULOUS CARS OF THE 1920s & 1930s
KIT CARS: CARS YOU CAN BUILD YOURSELF
MODEL CARS
RESTORING YESTERDAY'S CARS
VANS: THE PERSONALITY VEHICLES
YESTERDAY'S CARS

Bicycles
BICYCLE MOTOCROSS RACING
BICYCLE ROAD RACING
BICYCLE TRACK RACING
BICYCLES ON PARADE

Motorcycles
GRAND NATIONAL CHAMPIONSHIP RACES
MOPEDS: THE GO-EVERYWHERE BIKES
MOTOCROSS MOTORCYCLE RACING
MOTORCYCLE RACING
MOTORCYCLES ON THE MOVE
THE WORLD'S BIGGEST MOTORCYCLE RACE:
   THE DAYTONA 200

Other Specialties
BALLOONING
KARTING
MOUNTAIN CLIMBING
RIVER THRILL SPORTS
SAILBOAT RACING
SOARING
SPORT DIVING
SKYDIVING
SNOWMOBILE RACING
YESTERDAY'S FIRE ENGINES
YESTERDAY'S TRAINS
YESTERDAY'S TRUCKS

Lerner Publications Company
241 First Avenue North, Minneapolis, Minnesota 55401